D1403441

ADAM HAMILTON

Author of *Creed: What Christians Believe and Why*

THE
WALK

FIVE ESSENTIAL PRACTICES
OF THE CHRISTIAN LIFE

Leader Guide
by Clara Welch

Abingdon Press/Nashville

The Walk
Five Essential Practices of the Christian Life
Leader Guide

978-1-5018-9121-2

19 20 21 22 23 24 25 26 27 28—10 9 8 7 6 5 4 3 2 1
MANUFACTURED IN THE UNITED STATES OF AMERICA

CONTENTS

TO THE LEADER

Welcome! Thank you for accepting the invitation to serve as the facilitator for this study of *The Walk* by Adam Hamilton. You and your group of learners will journey together toward a greater understanding of what it means to walk with God.

During this six-session study Adam Hamilton invites readers to practice five spiritual disciplines that draw us closer to God. These five spiritual disciplines are:

- Worship and Prayer;
- Study (listening, paying attention, and Bible study);
- Serving;
- Giving; and
- Sharing.

This six-session study makes use of the following components:

- the book *The Walk* by Adam Hamilton,
- this Leader Guide, and
- a DVD with video segments for each of the six chapters in the book.

It will be helpful if participants obtain a copy of the book in advance and read chapter 1 before the first session. Each participant will need a Bible. A notebook or journal is also recommended for taking notes, recording insights, and noting questions during the study.

Session Format

Every group is different. These session plans have been designed to give you flexibility and choices. A variety of activities and discussion questions are included. As you plan each session, keep the session goals in mind and select the activities and discussion questions that will be most meaningful for your group.

You will want to read the section titled "Before the Session" several days in advance of your meeting time. A few activities suggest making some preparations in advance.

A key purpose of this study is to encourage participants to practice spiritual disciplines. The activities in "Getting Started" are designed to serve as a quick review of the spiritual discipline introduced in the previous session and to give participants an opportunity to share their experience of practicing this spiritual discipline. Watch your time here so you will have time for the in-depth study of the new spiritual discipline presented later in the session.

In many cases your session time will be too short to do everything that is suggested here.

Select ahead of time which activities best fit the personality of the group and decide how much time you want to allow for each part of the session plan.

The activities in "Wrapping Up" are designed to give participants the opportunity to reflect on the spiritual discipline presented in the session and to begin thinking about how they will practice this spiritual discipline going forward. For the Closing Prayer you may invite participants to pray the prayer at the end of the chapter in *The Walk*, or you may offer your own prayer.

Each session plan follows this outline.

- Planning the Session
  - ◊ Session Goals
  - ◊ Biblical Foundation
  - ◊ Before the Session

- Getting Started
  - ◊ Opening Activities
  - ◊ Leading into the Study
  - ◊ Opening Prayer

- Learning Together
  - ◊ Video Study and Discussion
  - ◊ Bible Study and Discussion
  - ◊ Book Study and Discussion
  - ◊ Optional Activity

- Wrapping Up
  - ◊ Closing Activity
  - ◊ Closing Prayer

Preparing for the Session

- Pray for the leading of the Holy Spirit as you prepare for the study. Pray for discernment for yourself and for each member of the study group.
- Before each session, familiarize yourself with the content. Read the book chapter thoroughly, make notes, and watch the video segment.
- Choose the session elements you will use during the group session, including the specific discussion questions you plan to cover. Be prepared, however, to adjust the session as group members interact and as questions arise. Prepare carefully, but allow space for the Holy Spirit to move in and through the material, the group members, and you as facilitator.

- Secure in advance a TV and DVD player or a computer with projection.
- Prepare the space so that it will enhance the learning process. Ideally, group members should be seated around a table or in a circle so that all can see each other. Movable chairs are best, because the group will often be forming pairs or small groups for discussion.
- Bring a supply of Bibles for those who forget to bring their own. Having a variety of translations is helpful.
- For each session you will also need a whiteboard and markers, a chalkboard and chalk, or an easel with paper and markers.

Shaping the Learning Environment

- Begin and end on time.
- Create a climate of openness, encouraging group members to participate as they feel comfortable. Remember that some people will jump right in with answers and comments, while others will need time to process what is being discussed.
- If you notice that some group members don't enter the conversation, ask them if they have thoughts to share. Give everyone a chance to talk, but keep the conversation moving. Try to prevent a few individuals from doing all the talking.
- Communicate the importance of group discussions and group activities.
- If no one answers at first during discussions, don't be afraid of pauses. Count silently to ten; then say something such as "Would anyone like to go first?" If no one responds, venture an answer yourself and ask for comments.
- Model openness as you share with the group. Group members will follow your example. If you limit your sharing to a surface level, others will follow suit.
- Encourage multiple answers or responses before moving on.

- Ask, "Why?" or "Why do you believe that?" or "Can you say more about that?" to help continue a discussion and give it greater depth.
- Affirm others' responses with comments such as "Great" or "Thanks" or "Good insight."
- Monitor your own contributions. If you find yourself doing most of the talking, back off so that you don't train the group to listen rather than speak up.
- Remember that you don't have all the answers. Your job is to keep the discussion going and encourage participation.

Managing the Session

- Honor the time schedule. If a session is running longer than expected, get consensus from the group before continuing beyond the agreed-upon ending time.
- Involve group members in various aspects of the group session, such as playing the DVD, saying prayers, or reading the Scripture.
- Note that the session plans sometimes call for breaking into smaller groups. This gives everyone a chance to speak and participate fully. Mix up the teams; don't let the same people pair up on every activity.
- Because many activities call for personal sharing, confidentiality is essential. Group members should never pass along stories that have been shared in the group. Remind the group members at each session: confidentiality is crucial to the success of this study.

1

WORSHIP AND PRAYER
A LIVING HALLELUJAH

Planning the Session

Session Goals

Through conversation, activities, and reflection, participants will:

- accept the invitation to walk with Christ;
- affirm the importance of worshiping in community; and
- commit to a discipline of individual worship through daily prayer.

Biblical Foundation

Psalm 95

Before the Session

- Set up a table in the room with name tags, markers, Bibles, and extra copies of *The Walk* if these will be needed.
- Have a whiteboard or chart paper and markers or a chalkboard and chalk, available for recording participants' responses.

- In preparation for the "Leading into the Study" discussion, draw a vertical line on a board or large sheet of paper to make two columns. In the first column write the heading, "What is a Christian?" In the second column write the heading "Characteristics."
- In preparation for the discussion "What Is Worship?" draw two vertical lines on a board or large sheet of paper to create three columns and write these three headings: *proskyneo*, *sebomai*, and *latreuo*.
- If you plan to do the "Optional Activity," have hymnals and/or worship songbooks available. You may want to recruit an accompanist.

Getting Started

Opening Activities

Greet participants as they arrive. Invite them to make a name tag and pick up a Bible and/or a copy of *The Walk* if they did not bring one.

Introduce yourself and share why you are excited about this study of *The Walk: Five Essential Practices of the Christian Life* by Adam Hamilton.

Invite each participant to introduce himself/herself and to respond to this question:

- What sparked your interest in participating in this group study of *The Walk: Five Essential Practices of the Christian Life* by Adam Hamilton? (Let participants know it is fine if some of the reasons are repeated.)

Housekeeping

- Share any necessary information about your meeting space and parking.
- Let participants know you will be faithful to the time and encourage everyone to arrive on time.

- Encourage participants to read the upcoming chapter each week and do any "homework" that may be suggested.
- You may want to invite participants to have a notebook, journal, or electronic tablet for use during the study. Explain that these can be used to record questions and insights as they read each chapter and to take notes during each session.
- Ask participants to covenant together to respect a policy of confidentiality within the group.

Leading into the Study

Invite participants to respond to the following two questions. Instruct them to call out the first ideas that come to mind. Recruit a volunteer to record responses on the board or large sheet of paper with the headings, "What is a Christian" and "Characteristics." Recruit another volunteer to serve as timekeeper. Limit the time for each question to two minutes.

First ask:

- What is a Christian?

Then ask:

- What are the characteristics of a Christian?

After the two lists have been compiled, invite participants to consider the group's responses and the process. Ask:

- Did you find it easy or difficult to answer these questions?
- Are there any common themes among the responses?

The focus for the first session is the spiritual discipline of worship, including prayer.

Opening Prayer

Loving God, thank you for walking with us. Thank you for inviting us to walk with you. Be with us as we learn together and grow in our understanding of what it means to be a Christian. In the name of your Son Jesus Christ, we pray. Amen.

Learning Together

Video Study and Discussion

Invite participants to consider these questions as they view the video:

- In the video, Adam Hamilton says that he wants "to walk with Jesus wherever he wants me to go." How can spiritual practices like worship and prayer make us better able to walk with Jesus?
- What does it look like in your life when you are spiritually winded or struggling?
- Hamilton describes two dimensions of each spiritual practice: things we do together and things we do individually. What is the relationship between these two? Why are both important?
- Describe your experience with daily prayer. How central is prayer in your life? How can you take steps toward more or deeper prayer, starting with saying "Thank you" to God?

Following the video invite volunteers to share their responses to the questions above.

Bible Study and Discussion—Psalm 95

Remind the group that during this study we will examine five spiritual disciplines.

Invite participants to turn to chapter 1 in *The Walk*. Call attention to the subtitle, "A Living Hallelujah" and Psalm 95 printed at the beginning of this chapter from the NRSV. Explain that Psalm 95 offers insight into the community worship of ancient Israel. The first phrase of the psalm, "O come, let us sing to the Lord," sets the tone. Lead the group in reading Psalm 95 together.

Reread the first two verses of Psalm 95 to the group and point out that these are a call to worship.

> *O come, let us sing to the* Lord*;*
> > *let us make a joyful noise to the rock of our salvation!*
> *Let us come into his presence with thanksgiving;*
> > *let us make a joyful noise to him with songs of praise!*

Ask:

- Do you come to worship God with joy and thanksgiving?
- With what other feelings have you come before God to worship?
- Is there value in coming to worship even when you have negative feelings or neutral feelings? Why or why not?

Reread verses 3 through 5 of Psalm 95 to the group:

> *For the LORD is a great God,*
> *   and a great King above all gods.*
> *In his hand are the depths of the earth;*
> *   the heights of the mountains are his also.*
> *The sea is his, for he made it,*
> *   and the dry land, which his hands have formed.*

Ask:

- What does this verse tell us about God's relationship with all creation? (We belong to God, like all creatures. God is our creator and ruler. All of creation is in God's hands.)
- How does remembering this relationship help us approach worship with joy, even when we are experiencing pain and crisis?

Reread verses 4 through 7 of Psalm 95 to the group:

> *O come, let us worship and bow down,*
> *   let us kneel before the LORD, our Maker!*
> *For he is our God,*
> *   and we are the people of his pasture,*
> *   and the sheep of his hand.*

Ask:

- Why does the psalmist give thanks and praise to God?
- What do these verses tell us about our relationship with God?
- Why do you give thanks and praise to God?

Call attention to Hamilton's observation that when we worship we are saying "Thank you!" and "I love you" to God. Hamilton describes this as "the essence of worship and the most basic form of prayer."

Book Study and Discussion

Metaphors for the Christian Life

Call attention to several metaphors found in Scripture for the Christian life: new birth, repentance, faith, and walking with Jesus. Invite participants to read Scripture passages where these metaphors are used, then refer to the introduction of *The Walk* where Adam Hamilton discusses the metaphor of walking with Jesus.

New Birth

Read these Scripture passages from the Gospel of John:

> *But those who did welcome him,*
> > *those who believed in his name,*
> *he authorized to become God's children,*
> > *born not from blood*
> > *nor from human desire or passion,*
> > *but born from God.*
> > > > > (*John 1:12-13*)

> *I assure you, unless someone is born anew, it's not possible to see God's kingdom.*
> > > > > (*John 3:3*)

Ask:

- What does the metaphor of new birth teach us about what it means to be a Christian?
- How does being "born anew" bring about a reorientation of our lives? (It is a reorientation away from love of the world to an orientation of love for God.)

Repentance—metanoia *(Greek)*

Read these Scripture texts from the Gospel of Mark and the Book of Acts:

> *After John was arrested, Jesus came into Galilee announcing God's good news, saying, "Now is the time! Here comes God's kingdom! Change your hearts and lives, and trust this good news!"*
>
> *(Mark 1:14-15)*

> *Peter replied, "Change your hearts and lives. Each of you must be baptized in the name of Jesus Christ for the forgiveness of your sins. Then you will receive the gift of the Holy Spirit."*
>
> *(Acts 2:38)*

Note that repentance sets in motion a series of changes. A change of mind leads to a change of heart, which leads to a change in behavior. Ask:

- What does the metaphor of repentance teach us about what it means to be a Christian?
- How does repentance bring about a reorientation of our lives? (*It is a reorientation away from living for self to living for God.*)

Faith—pistis *(Greek)*

Read Paul's words to the church in Rome:

> *"Because if you confess with your mouth 'Jesus is Lord' and in your heart you have faith that God raised him from the dead, you will be saved."*
>
> *(Romans 10:9)*

Ask:

- What does the metaphor of faith or trust in Christ teach us about what it means to be a Christian?
- How does our decision to place our faith in Christ reorient the way we live our lives?

Walking with God—akoloutheo *(Greek "to follow")*

Instruct participants to turn to the section of the introduction titled "Walking with God." Invite volunteers to read aloud the various Scripture passages included in this section. You may also want to ask participants if they are familiar with other Scripture passages about walking with God and invite them to share these. Then ask:

- What do these Scripture passages tell us about what it means to walk with the Lord? (You may want to list responses on a board or large sheet of paper.)
- How is the idea or image of walking with God meaningful to you?

Summarize Hamilton's points in the section titled "Out of Shape" including reasons why the practice of spiritual disciplines is important in the Christian life.

What Is Worship?

Invite participants to reference the section titled "What Is Worship?" as they participate in this discussion. Note the definition in the first paragraph: "Worship is the primary and appropriate response of the creature to the Creator."

Explain the meaning of the Old English word *woerthship* (worthship). Ask:

- How does this word add to your understanding of worship?
- Why is it important to worship in community?
- Why is it important to worship as an individual by yourself?
- What has been your experience of individual worship or private prayer? (Draw attention to Hamilton's "five-fold pattern of prayer" during this discussion.)
- How can you offer "the primary and appropriate response" to God through daily prayer?

Cultivate Gratitude

Share the idea of a "gratitude journal." Invite participants to suggest other ways to cultivate gratitude toward God. Ask:

- How has gratitude increased your happiness?
- What are you most grateful for? How do you incorporate thankfulness into your pattern of worship and prayer?
- What can you do to increase your gratitude in response to what you learned in chapter 1?

Invite participants to begin using a gratitude journal as one way to be more mindful of all that God has given them and how they can respond to it with thankfulness.

Optional Activity

"Precious Lord, Take My Hand"

In the section titled "Walking with God" Hamilton references Thomas Dorsey's hymn "Precious Lord, Take My Hand" (*The United Methodist Hymnal* No. 474). Invite participants to compile a list of hymns and songs about "Walking with God." This will include hymns and songs about following Jesus and Christian discipleship.

If you have a large group, suggest that participants work in pairs or small groups. Have a supply of your congregation's hymnals and worship songbooks available and suggest that participants may also look up songs on electronic devices.

Offer time for groups and individuals to share their findings. Read or sing the lyrics together. You may want to recruit an accompanist.

Wrapping Up

Closing Activity

Close the session by emphasizing the importance of daily prayer in the Christian life. (See section titled "Daily Prayer: Our Individual Worship" in *The Walk*.) Remind the group of Adam Hamilton's invitation for us to pray five times each day: once in the morning, once at each meal, and once at night.

Ask:

- How does this five-fold pattern of prayer compare with your current practice? Do you already pray at these times?
- If so, how might you renew or refocus your commitment to prayer?
- If not, what can you do to get started?

Invite each person to write down specific times he or she can pray each day, allowing time to share their thoughts and ideas once they have written them down.

As you close the session, encourage the group to pray five times each day during the coming week at the times they have identified. Commit to checking in with them at your next meeting to see how it's going. End with the following reminders:

- Be mindful of the ways to express gratitude to God;
- Practice the spiritual discipline of worship and daily prayer;
- Read chapter 2 of *The Walk*.

Closing Prayer

Pray the prayer at the end of chapter 1 together or pray your own prayer.

2

STUDY
THE IMPORTANCE OF LISTENING AND PAYING ATTENTION

Planning the Session

Session Goals

Through conversation, activities, and reflection, participants will:

- Consider the ways God speaks to us through general and special revelation;
- Explore different ways to hear God's voice through Scripture;
- Commit to practicing the spiritual discipline of listening for God's word.

Biblical Foundation

Psalm 19:1-4

Before the Session

- Set up a table in the room with name tags, markers, Bibles and extra copies of *The Walk* if these will be needed.

- Have a whiteboard or chart paper and markers or a chalkboard and chalk available for recording participants' responses.
- Have a Common English Bible, an NRSV Bible, and an NIV Bible available for the Bible Study and Discussion.
- This lesson plan offers two suggestions for the discussion about general revelation through the arts. If you would like to do Option A, bring in one or two pieces of visual art—perhaps a painting, photograph, sculpture, or a piece of fabric art.

Getting Started

Opening Activities

Greet participants as they arrive. If there are newcomers allow a short time for introductions.

Share any housekeeping items that need repeating. (See the list for session 1.) Remind participants to respect a policy of confidentiality within the group.

Leading into the Study

In his book *The Walk*, Hamilton presents several spiritual disciplines that guide and strengthen our walk with God. It will be helpful to begin the session by "checking in" and offering time for participants to briefly share their experiences of practicing the discipline that was presented in the last session. Encourage participants to respond with short answers so as not to take time away from the Bible Study and Book Study later in the session. If you have a large group, suggest that participants share in small groups of three to four people so that everyone who wants to share will have the opportunity.

Remind the group that in the last session we studied the spiritual discipline of worship and prayer, and realized the importance of worship both in community and as individuals. Ask:

- How has your experience of community worship strengthened your walk with God?

- How has your experience of individual worship through prayer strengthened your walk with God?
- How will you continue to practice the discipline of worship and prayer going forward?

Remind the group that the topic for the second session is the spiritual discipline of study, listening for God with an emphasis on Scripture reading.

Opening Prayer

Holy and loving God, thank you for walking with us. Thank you for revealing yourself to us as we walk with you. We pray that you will open our eyes and our ears so we may be mindful of what you are saying to us. Open our hearts to receive your word. In the name of your Son Jesus Christ, we pray. Amen.

Learning Together

Video Study and Discussion

Invite participants to consider these questions as they view the video:

- What is one thing you learned that you did not know before?
- Adam Hamilton describes the importance of listening to our Master's voice amid other voices that call to us. What other voices are out there that might be tempting but are ultimately dangerous? How can we attune our ears to recognize our Master's voice?
- When have you learned something about God from nature, the arts, or some other aspect of general revelation?
- Why is it important to read Scripture both together with others and on our own regularly?

Following the video invite volunteers to share their responses to the questions above.

Bible Study and Discussion—Psalm 19:1-4

Invite participants to read together Psalm 19:1-4 from the NRSV as printed in the section titled "Nature" in chapter 2.

Recruit two volunteers to read the same passage from the CEB and NIV while participants follow the text from the NRSV.

Ask:

- What differences in wording do you notice between these versions of Psalm 19:1-4?
- What do the heavens reveal to us about the glory and the nature of God? Responses may include:
  ◊ *God is dependable as evidenced in the cycle of day and night, sun and moon, and the seasons.*
  ◊ *God loves beauty as revealed in a sunrise or sunset.*
  ◊ *God is powerful as shown in a thunderstorm.*
  ◊ *God remembers his promise to us as revealed in the rainbow (Genesis 9:8-16).*
- What do other aspects of nature reveal to us about God? Responses may include:
  ◊ *Flowers reveal God's love of beauty.*
  ◊ *The mountains and ocean waves reveal God's strength.*
  ◊ *Butterfly wings reveal God's gentleness.*
  ◊ *The season of spring reveals God's faithful promise of hope.*
- When have you had a special experience of God's presence or a revelation of God's word to you while in nature?
- What significance is it that the Bible points to nature as a way of knowing God? What does this imply about the relationship between general revelation and special revelation?

Book Study and Discussion

In chapter 2 of *The Walk*, read the first paragraph in the section titled "General Revelation," which contains definitions of Revelation, General Revelation, and Special Revelation.

General Revelation

Call attention to Hamilton's four examples of General Revelation where we may experience God speaking to us:

- Nature
- The Arts
- Life Experiences and Other People
- Our own Conscience, Intuition, and Reason

Remind the group that the Bible Study and Discussion of Psalm 19:1-4 gave us the opportunity to explore ways God reveals God's self to us through nature.

Introduce a discussion of the ways God reveals God's self through the arts by reading Genesis 1:27: "God created humanity in God's own image" (CEB).

Share these three points:

- God is our Creator and God has blessed us with the gift of creativity.
- Sometimes God speaks to us when we engage in creative activity.
- Sometimes God speaks to us through the creativity of others.

Select one of the following two options and lead the group in an exploration of ways that God reveals God's self through the arts.

Option A

Bring in one or two pieces of visual art to show the group. See Before the Session for ideas.

Invite participants to view the art for a few minutes in silence and to open their minds and hearts to whatever God may be saying to them through this art. (If you brought in two pieces suggest that each participant choose to focus on one for this activity. You may also want to note that there are no "right" or "wrong" answers and it is fine if everyone does not sense God speaking to them through these particular pieces of art at this particular time.)

After participants have had time to contemplate the art, ask:

- What is God revealing to you through this art?
- What was this process of listening for God through art like for you?

<u>Option B</u>

Invite participants to describe a time when they experienced God speaking to them through the arts, including visual arts, music, poetry, dance, a movie, a theater production or another art form. If you have a large group, create small groups of three to five people for this discussion.

Special Revelation

Invite a volunteer to read the first paragraph in the section titled "Special Revelation." Call attention to three direct ways God has spoken to humankind in the past and continues to speak to humankind today:

- The Holy Spirit
- Scripture
- Jesus: God's Word in the Flesh

The Holy Spirit

Invite a volunteer to read the first paragraph of the section titled "The Holy Spirit."

Suggest that participants reference this section as they respond to the following questions. Ask:

- What examples does Hamilton give of times when he heard the Holy Spirit speaking to him?
- How can we be certain that what we hear is from the Holy Spirit?
- When have you heard the Holy Spirit speaking to you?
- What helped you determine that yes, this was the Holy Spirit?
- How did you respond?

Scripture

Hamilton highlights five ways we may read the Scriptures:

- Reading for Understanding
- Reading for Formation
- Praying the Scriptures
- *Lectio Divina*
- Bible Study with Others

(If there are participants in your group who are new Christians or who are new to Bible study, you may want to do the Optional Activity at this time. Then continue the session following option A, B, C, D, or E below.)

Lead your group in an exploration of the ways God speaks to us through the Scripture using one or more of the following options.

Option A

- Summarize the information in *The Walk* about Reading for Understanding.
- Encourage participants to try some of the Bible study tools that are available. Ask which of these tools they have tried before, and how they have found them helpful. Give the group an opportunity to explore how they might incorporate some of these tools into their Bible reading.

Option B

- Summarize the information about Reading for Formation.
- Encourage participants to ask themselves the three questions Hamilton mentions when they read Scripture for this purpose. Read 2 Timothy 3:14-17 with these questions in mind, and discuss your responses to each of Hamilton's questions.

Option C

Lead the group in an experience of Praying the Scriptures.

- Read Matthew 5:14-16 (printed in *The Walk* from the CEB) and the examples of prayers based on this text.

- Instruct participants to read Matthew 5:14-16 silently and to write a sentence prayer based on these verses. Distribute paper and pencils if needed.
- Invite volunteers to share their prayers.

Option D

Lead the group in reading a Scripture passage following the four acts or movements of *lectio divina* as explained in *The Walk*.

- Explain that the goal of reading Scripture in this way is communion with God.
- Explain the four movements of (1) reading, (2) meditation, (3) contemplation, and (4) prayer.
- Use Psalm 8:3-5, Psalm 119:105, or select another passage of Scripture.
- Read the passage and guide participants through the four acts.
- Invite participants to share insights or feelings after reading Scripture in this way.

Option E

- Summarize the reasons why Bible Study with Others is important for our Christian walk with God.
- Invite participants to share how group Bible study has helped them grow in the Christian faith.

Jesus: God's Word in the Flesh

Hamilton writes that,

> "When God sought to speak to the human race, to disclose who God is and who God calls us to be, he did not send a book, he sent a Person. Jesus was God's Word, God's message, wrapped in human flesh."

(The Walk, p. 60)

Ask:

- Why is this true?
- What does God reveal about God's self through Jesus?

Optional Activity

What Is the Bible

This Optional Activity is based on the opening paragraphs in the section titled "Scripture." Explain that the Bible contains different types of literature. Invite participants to reference the Table of Contents in their Bibles as you share the information below.

The Old Testament

Genesis through Deuteronomy:
- These first five books of the Bible are called the Torah or Pentateuch.

Genesis:
- Creation and the Flood
- Abraham and Sarah
- Isaac and Rebekah
- Jacob, Leah, Rachel, and their children
- Joseph and the Israelites in Egypt

Exodus through Deuteronomy:
- Moses
- The Israelites' escape from bondage in Egypt and journey through the wilderness to the edge of the Promised Land
- The Law that God gave to Moses and the Israelites on Mount Sinai to help them understand what it meant for them to be the people of God

Joshua through Esther:
- History books

Job through Song of Solomon:
- Books of Israel's poetry and wisdom

Isaiah though Daniel:
- God's word spoken through the Major Prophets

Hosea through Malachi:
- God's word spoken through the Minor Prophets

The New Testament

Matthew, Mark, Luke, John:
- The four Gospels—tell about the life, teachings, death, and resurrection of Jesus
- Matthew, Mark, and Luke are similar in nature and are called the Synoptic Gospels.
- Mark was the first Gospel to be written.
- John was the last Gospel to be written.

Acts:
- Tells about the Acts of the Apostles as they established the Christian church following the death and resurrection of Jesus
- Includes the story of Paul's conversion to become a follower of Christ

Romans through Philemon:
- Letters written by Paul (or attributed to Paul) to the early Christians

Hebrews through Jude:
- Letters by other apostles to the early Christians

Revelation:
- A prophetic and apocalyptic vision of the end time

Wrapping Up

Closing Activity

Remind the group of the ways God speaks to us through General Revelation and Special Revelation. If time permits, invite participants to share an insight or new learning they gained from this session.

In preparation for the next session encourage participants to:

- Continue to practice the spiritual discipline of Worship and Prayer by praying five times a day.
- Practice the spiritual discipline of study by reading Scripture, aiming for the goal of at least five verses of Scripture a day. Encourage the group to explore and use the various ways of reading the Bible.
- Read chapter 3 of *The Walk*.

Closing Prayer

Pray the prayer at the end of chapter 2 together or pray your own prayer.

3

SERVE
HERE I AM, LORD, SEND ME

Planning the Session

Session Goals

Through conversation, activities, and reflection, participants will:

- Discover the relationship between worship and service;
- Explore ways to love and serve God;
- Commit to serving God through acts of kindness to others.

Biblical Foundation

Romans 12:1-2

Before the Session

- Set up a table in the room with name tags, markers, Bibles and extra copies of *The Walk* if these are still needed.
- Have a whiteboard or chart paper and markers or a chalkboard and chalk available for recording participants' responses.

- Write the word *latreuo* on a large sheet of paper and display it in a prominent place in the room. You may want to embellish the letters. This will be used during the Bible Study and Discussion.
- Write the words "Love God" in the center of a board or large sheet of paper. This will be used for a "collage of words" during the Book Study and Discussion.

Getting Started

Opening Activities

Greet participants as they arrive. If there are newcomers allow a short time for introductions.

Share any housekeeping items that need repeating. (See the list for session 1.) Remind participants to respect a policy of confidentiality within the group.

Leading into the Study

Remind the group of the spiritual disciplines you have explored so far in your study: session 1: worship and prayer, and session 2: listening and paying attention.

Invite discussion of the following questions. If you have a large group suggest that participants share in small groups of three to four people so that everyone who wants to share will have the opportunity. Watch your time so you will have plenty of time for the study and discussion of chapter 3. Ask:

- Did you read at least five verses of Scripture a day since our last session? What parts of the Bible did you read?
- Since the last session, where else did you intentionally listen for God? (*Responses may include nature, the arts, or the Scriptures, for example.*)
- Did you practice a specific way of listening for God through Scripture, for example, Reading for Understanding, Reading for Formation, Praying the Scriptures, *Lectio Divina*, or Bible Study with Others?

- If yes, what did you discover?
- How do you plan to continue the practices of listening, paying attention, and study?

Remind the group that the topic for the third session is the spiritual discipline of serving, including acts of justice and kindness.

Opening Prayer

Holy and Loving God, thank you for inviting us to draw closer to you. Thank you for each person in this group. Be with us as we answer your call to love our neighbor and serve those in need. In the name of your Son Jesus Christ, we pray. Amen.

Learning Together

Video Study and Discussion

Invite participants to consider these questions as they view the video:

- In what ways is the practice of service important, even vital as we walk with Christ? How does it not only impact others, but shape your own heart and life?
- Adam Hamilton makes the point that God usually does not send angels, but sends humans to help others and make a difference. Where has God sent you to be an agent of healing and love? Where have you been served through someone else?
- What opportunities are there around you every day to serve someone? What opportunities can you recall from the past couple of days?
- Why is it so important to be attentive and open to interruptions as opportunities to serve? How can you open yourself more to such opportunities?

Following the video invite volunteers to share their responses to the questions above.

Bible Study and Discussion—Romans 12:1-2

Call attention to the Greek word *latreuo* written on the board or large sheet of paper. Note that this word connects with both worship and service. Hamilton observes,

> *Latreuo* is a Greek word that involves serving God through worship. This, as we have seen, is an important dimension of serving the Lord. But service is not only the act of worship, as important as that is. We are meant to serve God by doing his work and his will in this world.
>
> *(The Walk, p. 67)*

- What acts of worship are most meaningful for you? (*Responses may include prayer, singing, reading or listening to Scripture, listening to a sermon, placing money in the offering plate.*)
- How is offering worship to God also an act of service to God?

Invite two volunteers to read Romans 12:1-2, one from the CEB and one from the NRSV. Note the connection between "worship" and "service" shown by the different translations for the last part of verse 1.

CEB—"This is your appropriate priestly service."

NRSV—"which is your spiritual worship."

Draw attention to Paul's instruction "present your bodies as a living sacrifice" (verse 1).

Explain that in biblical times one of the responsibilities of the priests was to offer animal sacrifices on behalf of the people. This was an act of worship. Often these sacrifices were sin offerings made to bring about reconciliation between God and God's people.

When Jesus gave himself on the cross he became the final sacrifice, by giving himself for all the sins of all humankind. This brought an end to the need for animal sacrifices. Paul instructed the early Christians to present themselves as living sacrifices.

Ask:

- What words does Paul use to describe our "living sacrifice?" (*CEB—"holy and pleasing," NRSV—"holy and acceptable"*). You may add that the word "holy" is used to describe people, places, and actions that are related to God.

Invite a volunteer to read again Romans 12:2. Ask:

- What does Paul mean by the phrase "living sacrifice"? (*Verse 2 offers a clue. Responses may include: (1) We do not follow the ways of this world but we follow God's will. (2) We sacrifice or give up our self-centered desires to live according to God's desires for us.*)

Conclude this Bible Study and Discussion with these, or similar remarks: We may interpret Paul's phrase about being "transformed by the renewing of (our) minds" to mean an ongoing process. Through this process we "can figure out what God's will is" (CEB) and "discern what is the will of God" (NRSV). The practice of the spiritual disciplines we are learning about through this study of *The Walk* will help us in this process of figuring out and discerning.

Book Study and Discussion

Love God

Call attention to the board or paper with the words "Love God" written in the center (see Before the Session). Read Mark 12:28-31. Ask:

- What did Jesus say are the two most important commandments?
- What are the key words in this Scripture passage? (Responses will include: all, heart, being, mind, strength, and neighbor.)

Write these key words and phrases on the board or paper around the words "Love God." Write the words in a haphazard manner so the end result will be a collage of words. You may want to use different color markers and/or writing styles. You will add to this collage as the session progresses so leave room for more words and phrases.

Invite volunteers to read aloud the following Scripture passages that Hamilton references in the section titled "The Call To Serve." Depending on the time you have available for this activity you may want to select a few passages from the list or read all of them. Suggest that participants follow along in their own Bibles as the passages are read and to share any differences they notice between versions. After *each* passage is read ask the question below.

> Joshua 24:14-16 Proverbs 31:8-9
>
> Isaiah 1:17 Micah 6:8
>
> Matthew 7:12 Matthew 25:31-46
>
> Luke 4:16-19

- What key words and phrases in this Scripture passage help us understand what it means to Love God and Walk with God? (*Write the key words and phrases on the collage around the words "Love God" as instructed above. If words and phrases are repeated between the Scripture passages, place a star by them.*)

After the Scripture passages have been read and the collage is complete, share this quote from the end of the section titled "Serving God Together:"

> "This love is not a feeling, but a way of living and being."
>
> *(The Walk, p. 73)*

Invite participants to observe a few minutes of silence to think about this quote and the various words on the "Love God" collage. Then ask:

- What do these key words and phrases from Scripture say to you about your walk with God?

Kindness

Invite participants to turn to the section titled "Here I Am, Lord." Call attention to the Hebrew word *hesed* (or *chesed*) and note the various translations of this word in Scripture, including kindness, mercy, steadfast love, and covenant love. Note also that "undeserved" kindness, mercy, and love is called "grace."

Invite a volunteer to read Ephesians 2:8-10. Ask:

- What does Paul mean when he writes that "salvation is God's gift" (CEB)? (*We cannot earn salvation.*)

- How are we called to respond to God's gifts of grace, love, and salvation? (*have faith in Jesus Christ, love God and neighbor*)
- What "good things" (CEB) and "good works" (NRSV) are we called to do in response to God's love for us? (*Refer to the word collage "Love God" and the definitions of hesed during this discussion.*)

Read Proverbs 31:8-9. (If you read this earlier in the session let participants know that you are intentionally reading it again.) Ask:

- Who are the people in our community who cannot speak for themselves, who are destitute, vulnerable, needy and/or poor? (*You may want to record responses on a board or large sheet of paper. It is fine if the group begins with generalities, for example the homeless or unemployed. Guide your group to also identify specific needs in your area, for example, children who do not have enough food when school is not in session, lonely residents in a local nursing facility, a local rehab center that needs volunteers, or the person who lives next door or down the street.*)

Conclude the discussion of Proverbs 31:8-9 by encouraging participants to:

- pray about the needs that have been identified;
- ask God to show them where and/or how God is calling them to serve.

Read again Ephesians 2:10. Ask:

- How does Paul's statement that God planned for "good works...to be our way of life" (NRSV) influence your decisions and lifestyle?

Optional Activity

Divine Interruptions

Offer a brief summary of the information in the section titled "Being Open to Divine Interruptions." Ask:

- When have you stopped your work to pay attention to an interruption?
- How did this interruption provide an opportunity for you to show kindness to someone in the name of Christ?
- How did responding to this interruption draw you closer to God?
- What will you do going forward to help you be more open to responding to divine interruptions?

Wrapping Up

Closing Activity

Read this quotation from the section titled "A Daily Challenge":

- "If we're serious about walking with Christ, we'll cultivate the daily practice of serving God by serving others."

Highlight Hamilton's idea of letting the fingers on the left hand remind us to do five (at least) acts of kindness each week.

In preparation for the next session encourage participants to:

- Continue to practice the Spiritual Disciplines of Worship and Prayer (prayer five times a day) and Study (reading five verses of Scripture a day).
- Be intentional about practicing the Spiritual Discipline of Service by sharing love and kindness in the name of Christ, striving to extend at least five acts of kindness this week.
- Read chapter 4 of *The Walk*.

Closing Prayer

Pray together the prayer at the end of chapter 3 in *The Walk* or pray your own prayer.

4

GIVE
WHERE YOUR TREASURE IS…

Planning the Session

Session Goals

Through conversation, activities, and reflection, participants will:

- Understand Jesus' teachings about generosity;
- Explore how gratitude and purposeful living influence generosity;
- Examine their own feelings about living a life of generosity.

Biblical Foundation

Matthew 6:19-21

Before the Session

- Set up a table in the room with name tags, markers, Bibles, and extra copies of *The Walk* if these are still needed.
- Have a whiteboard or chart paper and markers or a chalkboard and chalk available for recording participants' responses.

- Write the heading "Generosity" on a board or large sheet of paper. This will be used during the Book Study and Discussion.
- If you plan to do the Optional Activity, write the heading "Ministries of Generosity" on a board or large sheet of paper.

Getting Started

Opening Activities

Greet participants as they arrive. If there are newcomers allow a short time for introductions.

Share any housekeeping items that need repeating. (See the list for session 1.) Remind participants to respect a policy of confidentiality within the group.

Leading Into the Study

Begin the session by offering a short time for participants to share their experiences related to practicing the discipline of service, the topic for the last session. Ask:

- Since the last session how did you share the love of Christ with others?
- Since the last session what acts of kindness did you extend to others?
- What, if any, frustrations did you experience as you practiced the discipline of service and sought to extend kindness?
- In what new ways did you serve Christ and others as a result of intentionally practicing this discipline?
- In what ways did serving others bring you joy?

Remind the group that the topic for this session is the spiritual discipline of giving: generosity toward God and others.

Opening Prayer

Holy and Generous God, we thank you for your abundant blessings and your amazing generosity toward us. We stand in awe of your gifts of overflowing grace, mercy, and love. Open our hearts that we may respond to your love with generosity toward others. In the name of your Son Jesus Christ, we pray. Amen.

Learning Together

Video Study and Discussion

Invite participants to consider these questions as they view the video:

- In the video Adam Hamilton describes the Bible and his wallet being in conflict. How do you experience this same conflict in your own life?
- Do you agree that our tax returns or our checkbooks are a reflection of our priorities and values? Why or why not?
- What does extraordinary generosity mean to you? How does such generosity shape our outlook on life and our walk with Christ?
- What is the relationship between the way we give together as a church and the way we give as individuals?
- Adam Hamilton says that when we die, the only things we can take with us are what we have given away. How can you invest more in these eternal treasures?

Following the video invite volunteers to share their responses to the questions above.

Bible Study and Discussion - Matthew 6:19-21

Invite a volunteer to read Matthew 6:19-21. This is printed at the beginning of chapter 4 in *The Walk* from the NRSV.

Also read verse 19 from the CEB: "Stop collecting treasures for your own benefit on earth, where moth and rust eat them and where thieves break in and steal them."

Ask:

- Why does Jesus say "Do not" or "Stop" storing up treasures for ourselves on earth? (*There are two key points here:*
  ◊ *a desire for money and material possessions may overpower our desire for a relationship with God.*
  ◊ *Jesus tells us to place our faith in God who is trustworthy, not in material possessions and money, which are easily lost.*)
- Have you had the experience of losing an earthly treasure to rust, breakage, theft, or other damage?
- If so, how did you feel about this loss?
- What are the "treasures in heaven" that Jesus calls us to "store up" (NRSV) or "collect" (CEB)? (*These relate to our growing faith and relationship with God and our acceptance of God's love for us.*)

Read again Matthew 6:21. Ask:

- Where is your treasure?
- Where is your heart?

You may want to suggest participants share responses to these two questions in small groups of three to four people. Remind the group of the covenant of confidentiality and also that sharing is voluntary/optional.

Book Study and Discussion

Hedonism

Call attention to the section of chapter 4 titled "Hedonism: Chasing after the Wind." Note that Hamilton highlights the contrast between the message we receive from Jesus and the message we receive from our culture. Read these contrasting messages as stated below.

Jesus said:

> "Take care! Be on your guard against all kinds of greed; for one's life does not consist in the abundance of possessions."
> *(Luke 12:15 NRSV)*

In contrast, Hamilton writes:

> "We live in a society where every voice around us is telling us just the opposite of Jesus' teaching—that our lives, in fact, *do* revolve around an abundance of stuff we own. Our culture tells us that, if we just had better, bigger, nicer, or cooler stuff, we'd be happier and more fulfilled."
>
> *(The Walk, p. 91)*

Ask:

- When have you acted on the belief that you would find happiness and fulfillment if you owned a certain item?
- What happened?

Remind the group of Jesus' words: "one's life does not consist in the abundance of possessions" (Luke 12:15).

Identify the "keys to the good life" Hamilton writes about in chapter 4:

- Gratitude;
- Living Purposefully;
- Generosity.

Gratitude: Giving Thanks for What You Have

This is the first key to the good life that Hamilton writes about in chapter 4.

Share Hamilton's story about wanting a newer model Mustang and note his declaration, "I'm so grateful for this car."

Invite participants to silently call to mind two things they own that (1) still serve their purpose and (2) they are dissatisfied with for some reason and would like to replace. (Examples may include home décor, an electronic device, or last year's style of clothing.)

Select a volunteer to begin and then go around the room with each participant in turn repeating these two sentences and filling in the blank: "I really like my _____. I'm so grateful for it." Do not stop to comment after each person.

Go around the group twice so participants may name two items. Let participants know it is fine if items are repeated and a person may also simply say "pass" instead of naming an item. If you have a large group, create smaller groups of five to seven people for this activity.

After you have gone around the group twice, ask:

- Do you feel differently about the items you mentioned after this exercise?
- How will adopting this attitude toward your possessions help you grow in gratitude?
- In what ways will adopting this attitude toward your possessions help you obey Jesus' instruction in Matthew 6:19-21? (*You may want to reread this Scripture printed at the beginning of chapter 4.*)
- How does gratitude affect our generosity toward others?

Remind the group that the Spiritual Discipline presented in chapter 1 is worship and prayer. Giving thanks to God is an important part of both our individual worship and our corporate worship.

Living Purposefully

This is the second key to living the good life that Hamilton writes about in chapter 4.

Invite discussion of these two questions, paraphrased from the first paragraph of the section titled "Living Purposefully." You may want to record key ideas on a board or large sheet of paper. Ask:

- What adds meaning to your life?
- What gives you fulfillment and a sense of purpose every day?

Read these two Scripture passages:

- John 14:6:
  Jesus answered, "I am the way, the truth, and the life."

- Matthew 22:37-39:
  "You must love the Lord your God with all your heart, with all your being, *and with all your mind. This is the first and*

greatest commandment. And the second is like it: You must
love your neighbor as you love yourself."

Ask:

- How do loving God and loving neighbor give our lives purpose?
- What is the relationship between this love and generosity?

Generosity

This is the third key to the good life that Hamilton writes about in
chapter 4.

*Note to the leader: As you lead this discussion be mindful that participants may
have a variety of strong feelings about parting with their money and material
wealth, some positive and some negative. Be sensitive to the fact that some
participants may not be able to make financial contributions as great as others
in the group. Also be mindful of participants who may struggle financially due
to job loss, medical bills, or other reasons. During the conversation you may
want to point out that God calls us to be generous not only with our money but
also with our love, compassion, time, and service.*

Share this quotation:

> "Because we were created in the image of a generous God,
> we were created for generosity to be the regular rhythm of
> our lives."
>
> *(The Walk, p. 103)*

Invite participants to refer to the sections of chapter 4 titled "God
Made Us for Generosity" and "Generosity and Joy" as they contribute to
this discussion.

Ask:

- What is generosity? You may want to record responses on a board
  or large sheet of paper.

Then ask Hamilton's questions from the section titled "Generosity
and Joy:"

- What's the rhythm of your life when it comes to generosity?
- Are you stingy with your tips?
- Do you try to get people down to the absolute rock bottom when negotiating a purchase, or do you find a fair price for both the seller and for you?
- Do you give generously when there is someone in need?
- Do you resent being asked for money, either by your church or by others?
- Or do you look forward to being asked and having the opportunity to give?

Note Hamilton's observation that there is a connection between our relationship with our wealth and our spiritual relationship with God. Ask:

- How does the practice of generosity help us grow deeper in our faith?

Optional Activity

Share Hamilton's story of the Bookmobile in the section titled "God Made Us for Generosity" (*The Walk*, p. 99-101) as an example of a ministry of generosity.

Ask:

- In what ministries of generosity have you participated? (*List these on a board or large sheet of paper.*)
- How do you feel about your experience of participating in these ministries?
- When have you been the recipient of someone's generosity?
- What ministries of generosity do you want to continue or begin, going forward?

Wrapping Up

Closing Activity

Note Hamilton's observation that generosity, like all the spiritual disciplines, is something we need to practice. Ask:

- What excites you about living a life of generosity?
- How does the practice of the spiritual discipline of generosity bring you joy?

In preparation for the next session encourage participants to:

- Continue to practice the spiritual disciplines of worship and prayer (session 1), study (session 2), and service (session 3).
- Commit to five acts of extraordinary generosity over the next month. Consider other ways in which the practice of generosity is or can become part of the regular rhythm of the group's lives.
- Read chapter 5 of *The Walk*.

Closing Prayer

Pray together the prayer at the end of chapter 4 in *The Walk*.

5

SHARE
GOING FISHING, REFLECTING LIGHT

Planning the Session

Session Goals

Through conversation, activities, and reflection, participants will:

- Consider what it means to be a witness for Christ;
- Reflect on why they are a follower of Christ;
- Affirm the importance of being a light for Christ in the world.

Biblical Foundation

Matthew 5:14-16

Before the Session

- Set up a table in the room with name tags, markers, Bibles, and extra copies of *The Walk* if these are still needed.
- Have a whiteboard or chart paper and markers or a chalkboard and chalk available for recording participants' responses.
- On a board or large sheet of paper write the question "What is Your Church Known For?" Under the question draw a vertical

line to make two columns. In one column write the heading "Positive" and in the other column write the heading "Negative."

- Have paper and pencils on hand for the "Elevator Speeches" portion of the Book Study and Discussion.

Getting Started

Opening Activities

Greet participants as they arrive. If there are newcomers allow a short time for introductions.

Share any housekeeping items that need repeating. (See the list for session 1.) Remind participants to respect a policy of confidentiality within the group.

Leading into the Study

Begin the session by offering a short time for participants to share their experiences related to practicing the spiritual discipline of generosity, the topic for the last session. Ask:

- Since the last session, how have you been generous toward others? (*Responses may include gifts of time and kindness in addition to gifts of money and material goods.*)
- Have you seen opportunities to extend extraordinary generosity in the past week?
- How has the practice of the spiritual discipline of generosity impacted your daily walk with God?

Remind the group that the topic for this session is sharing: witnessing to your faith.

Opening Prayer

Loving and Gracious God, we thank you for your presence in our lives. We thank you for the people who have shared your love and generosity with us, who have made your faithful presence known to us. We hear your call to be faithful witnesses and followers of Christ. We look to you for guidance, strength, and courage as we answer that call. In the name of your Son Jesus Christ, we pray. Amen.

Learning Together

Video Study and Discussion

Invite participants to consider these questions as they view the video:

- In the video Adam Hamilton describes sharing our faith as giving away what's been given to us. Who are the people responsible for your faith, and how did they witness to you?
- Hamilton observes that we naturally share what is important to us or what we see as good and positive. What is it about your faith that you feel driven to share with others?
- What is it that non-religious or nominally religious people tend to care about? How can we witness to people in a way that makes a connection with these desires and values?
- Do you tend to think of witnessing more as a one-time interaction, or as a long-term relationship? How can a relational focus shape your understanding of how you share your faith?
- Most of us find it easier to think about doing good works and letting those acts speak for us. Why is it important to share our faith with words too? How can you express your faith in words more directly and frequently?

Following the video invite volunteers to share their responses to the questions above.

Bible Study and Discussion—Matthew 5:14-16

Invite a volunteer to read Matthew 5:14-16.

Note that Hamilton writes, "When others see our good works, when we've demonstrated radical selfless love, this can draw others to Christ." (See section titled "What Is Your Church Known For?") Ask:

- According to Matthew 5:14-16, what is Jesus' strategy for evangelism? (*There are two ideas at work here. First, we let others see the things we do in the name of Christ in order to draw attention to God. Second, people respond to the good works by praising God.*)

Call attention to the word "you" in this Scripture passage and note that this word in English can be both singular and plural. Ask:

- Why is it important for people of faith to work together in community to be the light of Christ in the world?
- Why is it important for followers of Jesus to also be "light" as individuals?

You may want to continue this Bible Study and Discussion by reading Matthew 6:1-6. Draw attention to the contrast between Jesus' instructions in Matthew 5:14-16 to do "good things" in public and Jesus' instructions in Matthew 6:1-6 to "practice your religion" in secret. Ask:

- How does Jesus' teaching in Matthew 6:1-6 relate to Jesus' instructions in Matthew 5:14-16? (*One possibility is that the key issue is intent or motivation. Whenever we witness to our faith in public, it must be for the purpose of bringing glory to God and not to ourselves.*)

Book Study and Discussion

Summarize the opening section of chapter 5 titled "Testifying." Remind the group of the conversation between John Wesley and Peter Bohler, and Bohler's advice to Wesley: "Preach faith till you have it; and then, because you have it, you will preach faith."

Ask:

- What did Peter Bohler mean when he said this to John Wesley?
- When have you found this to be true in your own life?
- How often do you consult online reviews when you are making decisions about restaurants, movies, services and products?
- How strongly do these reviews influence your decision?

- How did the reviews of others, either online or in person, influence your decision to attend the church your currently attend?

Invite a volunteer to read the last paragraph of the section titled "The Power of Reviews."

Ask:

- How does the image of the church as the body of Christ enhance your understanding of what it means for the church to be a witness for Christ in the world?
- What talents and abilities has God given you that enable you to participate in your church's ministries of witness and outreach?

Call attention to the board or paper with the question "What is Your Church Known For" and the columns labeled "Positive" and "Negative" (see Before the Session). Ask the following questions, and record responses in the appropriate column:

- What are the positive things your church is known for? (*Encourage participants to consider both on-site and off-site ministries and attitudes.*)
- What are the negative things your church is known for? (*In other words, is there anything about your church that would discourage or prevent someone from attending?*)

Discuss your responses using the following questions:

- What can your church do to turn the negatives into positives in order to be a stronger witness for Christ in your community?
- In addition to the items already listed under "Positive," is there anything else you would like your church to be known for?
- What can you do to help make that happen?
- Why is it important to be a witness for Christ in your community?

Elevator Speeches

Instruct participants to turn to the section of chapter 5 titled "Invitational, Incarnational Living." Call attention to Karl Barth's summary of the Christian faith: "Jesus loves me this I know, for the Bible tells me so." (*The Walk*, p. 132). Then invite them to read Adam Hamilton's short "elevator speech," his testimony about what his faith means to him (*The Walk*, pp. 132-134).

Distribute paper and a pencil to anyone who does not have these with them. Invite participants to write down their responses to the following questions in preparation for writing their own elevator speech, their short summary of the Christian faith. Let them know they will have the opportunity to share responses if they wish to after you have asked all the questions. Allow time between each question for participants to write. Ask:

- How would you summarize the Christian faith in seven words or less?
- What do you believe about God and Jesus Christ? (*If participants struggle with this question, suggest that they identify three or four beliefs they feel are the most important to them.*)
- How does faith in Christ make a difference in your life?
- Why are you a Christian?
- Who is Jesus to you?
- What statements about your faith would you include in your elevator speech to share Christ with someone else?

You may want to offer time for participants to begin writing their speeches. Invite volunteers to practice their speech in front of the group. Then encourage them to finish their elevator speech before your next session.

Optional Activity

Be a Light for Christ

Lead the group in the Bible Study and Discussion of Matthew 5:14-16 before doing this Optional Activity. Remind the group that Jesus calls us to be a "light" both in community with other followers and as individuals.

Explain that the purpose of this activity is to plan a project that participants in the group may do together as a way of being the light of Christ and witnessing to God's love and faithfulness in your community.

Begin by inviting the group to brainstorm ideas for ways they may work together to be the light of Christ. Examples include: visiting a nursing home or hospital, purchasing groceries and delivering them to a local food bank, spending time with children in a community center, serving a meal in a soup kitchen, and purchasing and delivering items to a homeless shelter.

After the list is complete, instruct the group to select one project to carry out. If you have a large group, create smaller groups of four to eight people and invite each small group to select a project. It is fine if some groups select the same project.

Allow time for each group to make plans for carrying out the project. This will include selecting a day and time and also delegating responsibilities like contacting a facility and driving.

Encourage the group(s) to complete the project before the next session if possible. Let participants know they will have the opportunity during the next session to share their experience if they completed the project or to update the group about their plans if the project is still in progress.

Wrapping Up

Closing Activity

Remind the group of the title of chapter 5, "Share: Going Fishing, Reflecting Light." Ask:

- Why is it important to be a witness for Christ in our daily life?
- In what ways do you feel God calling you to go fishing and reflect light as a witness for Christ?

In preparation for the next session encourage participants to:

- Continue to practice the spiritual disciplines of worship and prayer (session 1), study (session 2), service (session 3), and giving (session 4).

- Write and practice their "elevator speech" so they will be ready to share their faith with someone else.
- Commit to inviting at least five people to invite to church over the next year, and take steps toward making the first of those invitations.
- Read chapter 6 of The Walk.

Closing Prayer

Pray together the prayer at the end of chapter 5 in *The Walk.*

6

THE FIVE PRACTICES FROM THE CROSS

Planning the Session

Session Goals

Through conversation, activities, and reflection, participants will:

- Discover the connection between Jesus' last words from the cross and the five essential Christian practices highlighted in *The Walk*;
- Reflect on how the intentional practice of these five spiritual disciplines has strengthened their walk with God;
- Commit to the continued practice of these spiritual disciplines.

Biblical Foundation

The "seven last words" of Jesus from the cross as recorded in:

- Matthew 27:45-50
- Mark 15:33-37
- Luke 23:32-43

- Luke 23:44-46
- John 19:25b-27
- John 19:28-30

Before the Session

- Set up a table in the room with name tags, markers, Bibles, and extra copies of *The Walk* if these are still needed.
- Have a whiteboard or chart paper and markers or a chalkboard and chalk available for recording participants' responses.
- Write the Biblical Foundation Scripture references listed above on a board or large sheet of paper for use during the Bible Study and Discussion.
- If you plan to do the Optional Activity have paper and pencils on hand for anyone who may need them.

Getting Started

Opening Activities

Greet participants as they arrive. Share any housekeeping items that need repeating. (See the list for session 1.) Remind participants to respect a policy of confidentiality within the group.

Leading into the Study

Begin the session by offering a short time for participants to share their experiences related to practicing the Christian practice of witnessing or sharing the faith, the topic for the last session. Ask:

- Since the last session, in what ways did you witness to your faith and share Christ's love with others?
- Did you have the opportunity to share your "elevator speech" and if so, how did that go?
- If any participants did the Optional Activity for session 5, "Be a Light for Christ" invite the group(s) that completed their project to share their experiences. Invite groups that are still working on their project to give an update on their progress.

Remind participants that Jesus calls us to be light to the world both individually and collectively as the body of Christ.

Introduce the topic for this session by reading the three Session Goals.

Opening Prayer

Loving and Gracious God, thank you for life and the many ways you bless our lives. Thank you for Jesus, who showed us by example how to walk with you. Guide and direct our steps as we practice the spiritual disciplines of worship and prayer, Bible study and listening, service, giving generously, and witnessing. Walk with us as we seek to be faithful followers of Jesus Christ. In his name we pray. Amen.

Learning Together

Video Study and Discussion

Invite participants to consider these questions as they view the video:

- What is one thing you learned from this session that you didn't know before?
- Adam Hamilton mentions that "in order to breathe or speak, the [crucifixion] victims needed to pull themselves up by the nails piercing their wrists, resulting in excruciating pain. What does that say about the importance of what Jesus said?
- As you consider how Jesus embodies the five essential spiritual practices on the cross, which do you find most compelling and inspiring? Why?
- How do Jesus' words on the cross reflect his lifelong commitment to the five practices we've been considering throughout this study?
- How has this study helped you grow in faith? How will you carry these things forward in the coming weeks and months?

Following the video invite volunteers to share their responses to the questions above.

Bible Study and Discussion

Explain that the setting for chapter 6 of *The Walk* is the crucifixion of Jesus. Note that Hamilton connects the "seven last words" Jesus spoke from the cross with the five essential Christian practices highlighted in *The Walk*.

Call attention to the board or paper with the list of Scripture passages that are the Biblical Foundation for this session (see Before the Session). Explain that these Scripture passages record the "seven last words" of Jesus from the cross.

Recruit six volunteers to read these Scripture passages. Allow time for each reader to locate his or her assigned Scripture text before the reading begins.

Matthew 27:45-50	Luke 23:44-46
Mark 15:33-37	John 19:25b-27
Luke 23:32-43	John 19:28-30

Instruct participants to:

- listen attentively as each Scripture passage is read;
- imagine what it would have been like to be a bystander in the crowd on the day of Jesus' crucifixion.

Then announce each Scripture reference in turn, invite the volunteer with that passage to read, and observe a few minutes of silence after each reading. After all the Scripture texts have been read, ask:

- What was this experience of hearing the last words of Jesus from the cross like for you?

Book Study and Discussion

This Book Study and Discussion has five sections corresponding to the five Christian practices highlighted in *The Walk*. The Wrapping Up activity is based on the last section of chapter 6, "A Divine Drama, Enacted for Us."

Worship and Prayer

Invite participants to turn to the section of chapter 6 titled "Worship…Prayer."

Note that the Gospels of Matthew and Mark record Jesus' heartfelt prayer from the cross, "My God, my God, why have you forsaken me?" (Psalm 22:1a, Matthew 27:46, Mark 15:34 NRSV). Call attention to the fact that prayer was a vital part of Jesus' daily life and highlight examples mentioned in this section of chapter 6. Ask:

- What does Jesus' prayer life teach us about Jesus?
- What does Jesus' prayer life teach us about prayer?
- What do we learn about Jesus from the fact that he prayed Psalm 22:1 as he experienced suffering on the cross?
- When have you expressed feelings of abandonment to God in prayer? (*You may want to invite participants to share responses to this question in pairs or groups of three.*)
- Why do we turn to God in prayer even when we feel God has abandoned us? (*We know on a deep level that God has not abandoned us. God wants us to share all of our feelings. God hears and accepts our prayers. We can pray with faith and assurance that God will deliver us.*)
- How has the practice of prayer strengthened your walk with God?

(*The Optional Activity offers the opportunity for participants to write their own prayers using Psalm 22 as a guide.*)

Study…Scripture

Invite participants to turn to the section of chapter 6 titled "Study…Scripture." Remind the group that Jesus recited Scripture from the Psalms when he cried out in prayer, "My God, my God, why have you forsaken me?" (Psalm 22:1a NRSV). Jesus also recited a verse from the Psalms when he gave himself, body and spirit, to God.

> *Into your hand I commit my spirit.*
> *(Psalm 31:5a NRSV)*

> *"Father, into your hands I commend by spirit."*
> *(Luke 23:46 NRSV)*

Jesus was well versed in the texts of the Old Testament. He would have learned Scripture from the rabbis, at the synagogue, and from his parents. Hamilton points out that he learned Psalm 31:5 from Mary, his mother, as a bedtime prayer when he was a child.

Ask:

- What bedtime prayers did you learn as a child?
- How were these prayers also statements of faith for you?
- Who told you Bible stories and taught you passages of Scripture when you were a child?
- When did you begin to study the Scriptures on your own?
- What passages of Scripture do you recite when you are in a time of crisis?
- How do these passages offer you help and hope during difficult and challenging times?
- What does it mean to you that Jesus quoted Scripture from the cross? Responses may include:
  - ◊ *It shows Jesus' humanity. He relied on God just as we need to.*
  - ◊ *It reinforces the importance of learning and memorizing Scripture.*
  - ◊ *Jesus showed by example the relevance of the Bible in our daily lives.*
- How has the practice of Bible study strengthened your walk with God?

Serving Others

Invite participants to turn to the section of chapter 6 titled "Serving Others."

Share these words of Jesus from the cross regarding the care of his mother as recorded in the gospel of John:

- To Mary: "Woman, here is your son" (John 19:26).
- To his disciple John: "Here is your mother" (John 19:27).

Read John 3:16 and call attention to the word "everyone." Share these key points:

- Jesus came to serve all humankind. By his suffering and death on the cross he opened the door to salvation for "everyone."
- Jesus calls us to follow in his footsteps and reach out in love and service to all people.
- When Jesus looked down from the cross to his mother and disciple, he issued a specific call for us to care for our parents and our families. This may be interpreted as a call to serve all parents and families. Hamilton writes, "I hear him calling all of us to care for those who are not our parents *as if they were* our parents."

Ask:

- In what ways do you care for and honor your parents? (*This is an especially significant question for people who are caring for aging parents. Be mindful that children of aging parents may experience feelings of guilt if distance, demanding jobs, or other circumstances prevent them from caring for aging parents as they would like to.*)
- Are there people around you that Jesus is calling you to care for as if they were your own mother or father?
- How has participation in acts of service strengthened your walk with God?

Generosity... Giving

Invite participants to turn to the section of chapter 6 titled "Generosity...Giving." Read John 19:28: "I am thirsty."

Ask:

- What new insights have you gained about Jesus' self-giving love from reading this section of chapter 6?

- When have you made sacrifices for another person out of love for that person?
- When have you been the recipient of someone's sacrificial love?
- How has the practice of self-giving love and generosity strengthened your walk with God?

Witnessing to the Gospel

Invite participants to turn to the section of chapter 6 titled "Witnessing to the Gospel."

Read these two of the "last seven words" from the cross:

> *Father, forgive them; for they do not know what they are doing."*
>
> *(Luke 23:34 NRSV)*

> *"Truly I tell you, today you will be with me in Paradise."*
> *(Luke 23:43 NRSV)*

Invite a volunteer to read the last paragraph in the section of chapter 6 titled "Witnessing to the Gospel." Ask:

- Why is forgiveness a powerful way to witness to our faith and draw others to Christ?
- How can you embody Christ's desire and action to seek out and witness to all people?
- How has the practice of the witnessing and sharing your faith strengthened your walk with God?

Optional Activity

Write a Psalm or Prayer

Invite participants to turn to Psalm 22 in their Bibles. Lead the group in the Book Study and Discussion for the part of this session plan titled *Worship...Prayer.* Continue the discussion with these two questions. Ask:

- What verses in Psalm 22 are cries for help? (*Examples are verses 1, 11, and 19-21a.*)

- Which verses in Psalm 22 are statements of faith? (*Examples are verses 3-5 and verse 24.*)

Invite participants to use Psalm 22 as a guide and write their own psalm or prayer that includes both expressions of abandonment and expressions of faith in God. Offer the option for participants to work individually, in pairs, and in small groups. Invite volunteers to read their psalm or prayer to the group.

Wrapping Up

Closing Activity

A Divine Drama, Enacted for Us

Read John 19:30 NRSV: "It is finished" or "It is completed" (CEB).

Note that with this final statement Jesus is proclaiming, "I've completed the mission!" Through his suffering and death on the cross Jesus finished the work God called him to do. Now all humankind may experience forgiveness, salvation, and new life through the risen Christ. One way we experience new life in Christ and a closer walk with God is through these five essential Christian practices of worship and prayer, study, serving, giving, and sharing.

Encourage participants to continue to these practices. Ask:

- How will you commit to making the practice of these spiritual disciplines part of your daily life?
- How has this study of *The Walk* impacted your daily walk with God?

Offer your own closing remarks about this course.

Closing Prayer

Pray together the prayer at the end of chapter 6 in *The Walk*.